LINDA GOODMAN'S LOVE POEMS

This book was lovingly protected
by *Kathleen Hyde*
of H. & R.

Linda Goodman's
Love Poems

LEVELS OF LOVE AWARENESS

HARPER & ROW, PUBLISHERS

NEW YORK

Cambridge London
Hagerstown   Mexico City
Philadelphia   São Paulo
San Francisco 1817 Sydney

Verses by Marilyn Monroe taken from *Marilyn: The Untold Story* by Norman Rosten. New York: New American Library, 1973. Reprinted by permission.

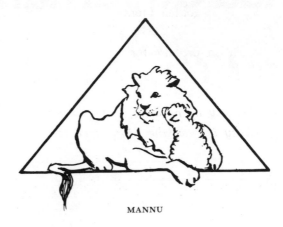

MANNU

Some of the verses in this book are from *Venus Trines at Midnight,* published in 1970 by Taplinger Publishing Co., Inc.

Designed by Lydia Link

Library of Congress Cataloging in Publication Data

Goodman, Linda.
   Linda Goodman's love poems.
   1. Love poetry, American. I. Title. II. Title:
Love poems.
PS3557.0584L6   811'.5'4   79–2731
ISBN 0–06–011643–9

80 81 82 83 84 10 9 8 7 6 5 4 3 2

for
Eleanor Boardman d'Arrast

magnetic actress, beautiful woman
golden Lioness

with a promise for tomorrow

"... *a quality of miracles, often forgotten, is*
the quality of ... the unexpected."

A continuing thank you

to Bill Webb
the skeptical Lion

who started it all with
a typical Leonine lecture
written in a letter dated
November 20th, 1968

". . . and so, you see, astrology is only one of several vocabularies, like music and art, that help us understand each other. But it's a singularly poetic language, with unique expression for some of the rhythms in our lives. I want to learn more about it—not to become an astrologer—but to become a better poet. I like its sweep, its broad symbolisms, the fact that it's such an ancient old thing that hasn't changed for millennia. Poetry! Poetry! Poetry!"

with Everlasting Love

I dedicate this
and all my future books
to "my sneaky guru"
Aaron Goldblatt

who has patiently, throughout all incarnations, guided
my creative efforts and spiritual enlightenment with
the infinite gentleness and wisdom of a Master Avatar;
and who has been . . . is now and ever shall be . . .
responsible for all my miracles . . . every single one
of them manifested only through his faith.

"Be not forgetful to entertain strangers, for
thereby some have entertained angels, unawares."

HEBREWS 13:2

"My children, errors will be forgiven. In our obsession
with original sin, we do often forget . . . original innocence."

POPE INNOCENT, OF ASSISI
15th Century A.D.

Contents

Song of the Ram

Spring may surprise me this year

I might actually literally find myself
on the Champs Élysées
with nothing to do but make love with you
in an attic room overlooking the Seine
or lying on the grass in the Bois de Boulogne

and suddenly, I'll notice it's April!

or I could just as easily wake up in the Highlands
drenched in an uncanny, golden glow
mingled with the spray of a fine Scottish mist
like the rain I ran through
in a flash of déjà vu
one day at an airport in the mountains

I'll spend lazy hours
shopping for a haunted old castle to live in
since I just won the Pulitzer prize
you'll be reading to me from Robert Burns
under Edinburgh skies

and suddenly, I'll remember it's April!

I might fly down the aisle
of a wildflower church in the Alps
ringing its bells for joy

and it's possible I'll win the Irish Sweepstakes
the same day my musical opens on Broadway
with floodlights and stars
like a gigantic Mike Todd production

or be born again — singing
in some little cemetery
taking its time
out west

    Spring owes me something

so far, she's pulled off a few splendid sparklers
a plump rosy angel who stayed for a while
      a make-believe tree house
and once, a shiny gold ring

but not a real Block Buster Sky Rocket miracle
like she always promised

    maybe this year, unexpectedly

Taurus

is it you?

or is it just that I've made you wear those love robes
I've been saving
since the days when my sand castles
were big enough to walk around in
and strong enough to stand against the tides?

I can't remember who first said
that "what you don't know can't hurt you"
but what's-his-name was wrong

supposing I climb all the way to the top of the tree
and then find out

it's not really you

how do I get back down again
all by myself?

I've always been afraid of heights

someone once said — I believe it was Sinatra or McKuen
that being a loner and being lonely
                         are not the same thing

    well, I don't know . .

I guess it's a safe enough answer to give
when people probe into your life style
at least it cuts off curiosity
from friends, strangers, and enemies
                              . . . sometimes one person
                              can be all three

I walked home this morning about 2:00 A.M. or so
which is kind of late to stroll Broadway
                         even for a loner

        it was raining

and all the taxis had disappeared, as usual
but I wasn't really lonely
                or even afraid of muggers
by that hour, they're home in the sack
or hanging around Howard Johnson's, drinking coffee

    New York muggers are a spoiled bunch

with millions of victims to pick from
they can afford to be choosy about working conditions
and who wants to hack out a living in a drizzle?

    they have a lot in common
                with Manhattan cabbies

it was good to have the Great White Way all to myself
I love to walk in the rain
it's like stepping into a giant shower
I always feel like singing
                and scrubbing my mind with Ivory soap

what is that thing in the air
that makes the pavements smell fresh and sweet

                        when they're wet?

I drank it in this morning
through my nose and my skin and my soul
while the moisture-drenched breeze
                        blew affectionately through my hair
and tangled my mind
into little wispy cobwebs of nostalgia

rain smells better on the grass, of course
in a small town, or in the country
where they still have happy, healthy trees

I remember that much
after twelve years in Fun City

                .. and I remember other things

oh! it was marvelous, the times it rained
                        when I was a child
I could put on my red-and-white-striped swim suit
run outside and splash through the puddles
                        at the curbs
squint my eyes, and tilt my head back
let the rain fall on my face
                open my mouth to drink the drops
and sniff that ozone smell
until I felt like screaming with joy
just to be alive
with maybe chocolate pudding for supper

it's not much like that anymore

for one thing, now I know
that chocolate, especially Rocky Road ice cream
clogs up the body's freeways
                    and considerably shortens life

I mean, I'll never be the same
since reading *Sugar Blues* .. by Bill Dufty

Aries Gloria Swanson's friend — and husband

                              sometimes one person
                              can be both

besides, if I had slushed, barefoot
this morning, through the puddles at the curbs
throwing back my head to drink in the raindrops

the narcotics squad

would have appeared out of nowhere
and hauled me in as a junkie

getting high on life — and drugs — is so similar
people can't always tell the difference at a distance

still, little spurts of chlorophyll
managed to make it this A.M., somehow, through the smog
soaking my senses, and tugging at my heart

                         as it always does

with the old, familiar call
of wild, impossible dreams and allelujah choruses
or maybe a miracle tomorrow, on a windswept hill!

and I felt that same delirious surge
of uncontrollable, indefinable happiness

I felt as a child

it lasted until I remembered the question
my driving instructor asked me
                    in Colorado last week

                        "why are you lonely?"

who's lonely?

            these are raindrops
            not tears .. on my cheek

isn't it wonderful that we have all that traffic at the corners?

> when we cross a street
> at an intersection
> and the cars streak by
> threatening sudden danger
> you reach out
> to grab my hand
> and hold it tightly

till we're safely on the other side

> then you let go
> gently
> reluctantly
> not right away

maybe that's why I always run against the light

> it's the only time we touch

the odd-shaped things I save, that smell and feel of us . . .

>a crumpled book of matches from the pizza place
>some wilted flowers, picked outside the door
>you couldn't enter

a bleached and crooked twig
washed ashore at that spot on the sand
where you first said you were lonely

>and surprised me into tears

a hotel room key, stuffed inside an airline ticket envelope

>a button you lost from your coat
>(who sewed a new one on, I wonder?)

I guess you saved the bird verse
and the memory of my last smile
>they take so little room in your scrapbook

most people love with restraint
as if they were someday to hate

we hated gently, carefully
as if we were someday to love

and now that you're gone
I'm free to cry at last
from the knowing
that I will be lonely for you
and you for me
through all the eternities before us

      but how much more so
      down here below
standing on the street where you left me

Follow That Star in the East, Officer

       were you there at the miracle of Woodstock?

the "third largest city" in New York State
surrounded by tiny rivers of hate
conceived in magic
born in music
and rocked in fields of alfalfa, baby

       were you there on the highway called Happy?

where the Jefferson Airplane streaked through the sky
exploding like a comet over Philippine Pond
while the cattle were lowing and roaming around
diggin' the sound
and the Wise Men rode on a Day-Glo bus

       Oh, come along with us
       and make the scene
       where Groovy Way meets Gentle Path
       at the intersection of Freedom
       and we'll all take a bath in milk and honey

come along now
and we'll reach for a song
we'll drink up a cupful of green meadow grass
or some rain on the rocks
and we'll find us a bed near the Grateful Dead

girl, if you go, I'll tell you true
the road's not straight

but just you wait
till you see the view
from the top of yourself

were you there at the miracle of Woodstock?
where the hazy smoke of Uranus dreams
softened the cries
of Melanie by the Mountain
did you drown with Joan in cool Sweetwater
to the piper's patter of Blood, Sweat and Tears

were you there?
did you care
when Arlo jumped clear over the Moon?

hey, diddle diddle, that cat and his fiddle
he turned on the stars not a wish too soon

did you see the horizons of multitudes?
wearin' rainbow robes and muddy boots
where Country Joe shared his Fish in the stable
with a couple of loaves from Max's Farm
and, man, it poured down all that bread
on all those beautiful people
like it did before
way up in the hills
when everybody shared his picnic basket
at that great Jerusalem love-in

oh, were you there when we rang the bells
of Woodstock?
so Richie Havens could hear us pray
while Janis flew high on the Milky Way
on a round-trip ticket to tomorrow?

girl, did you throb
to the chant of love me
touch me — heal me
feel me turn to gold
beneath soggy tents of plenty?

Oh, girl, did you feel me turn to gold?
then let it be told
that the sermon was preached with Creedence
at that Clearwater Revival — so fine
in the Year of our Lord
nineteen hundred and sixty-nine

did you catch the sight of Jimi and Tim?
takin' up a collection of warm
while the choir sang true
with an Incredible String Band
that wrapped your head in swaddling blankets

        were you there at the miracle of Woodstock?
where the Canned Heat burned
around the Butterfield Blues
eggin' on the Quill to call Santana
and spill more chords on Sly
so the Family Stone could pass the laughter
for Ten Years After

        how many Bulls kissed a Moon Child's eyes
        near the tree
        where the Ram lay down with the Lion
        and the Goat learned to talk with the Virgin
to the echo of a hundred guitars
as the Twins touched Venus on the way to Mars

        were you there with the many
when they saw the Who?
did it tremble you
to hear Johnny Winter come wailin' through
a summer sky
tossin' midnight moods to Bert and Ravi
did you wonder why it made you cry?

oh, how many ballads do you think were sung
by Keef and McDonald
for the love of Crosby, Stills, Nash and Young
and how many babies were bundled in sighs
to the rhythm of Sebastian's rock-a-byes
cradled by The Band that filled this big land
of the rocket's red glare
with LOVE bursting in air
to give proof through the night
and by dawn's early light
that the message was there

so far out of sight
it left your mind
way behind
     your soul

     were you there at the miracle of Woodstock?
when five hundred thousand Aquarian hearts
whispered a secret from one to another

     "There's a lot of us here
     and if we're all gonna make it
     we'd better remember
     each guy is our brother"

     so . . .

Peace, man, Peace

oh, tidings of great joy!

     oh

Peace, man, Peace

And Your Eyes Shall Be Opened

we could never recall the exact moment
perhaps it was that transcendental morning
                        . . maybe sooner, maybe later

when the veils were torn away
from our sleeping eyes
and our thirst was quenched with flooding waters

no earthly wisdom offered a reason
for two souls to so leap up in such unison
and follow a then unseen star

like two curious pilgrims
we heard a strange music, as we walked together
each stopping to wait
                when one fell behind in confusion
with a tenderness and understanding
foreign to our fiery spirits
        until finally, our wills blended so completely
the blending shamefully had to be covered
with little hurts and lies

                        to protect it

from the hungry and envious tigers
ready to attack it with stormy, mortal passions

do you not yet see
how those robes we wore, of pain dyed in pride
clashed with the brilliant colors of our auras?

        ah! we were truer naked

never mind how vulnerable

Air Sign Rejected

before you leave

> give me your hand again, for just one foolish moment

> I'll race you to the Moon!
> The cold night wind
>   will blow the cobwebs from your soul
> and I promise we'll be back by noon

ah, but wait ...
it's much too late for you to race through space

> this you tell me with the sad and empty eyes
> of one who knows the Moon's too far away
> to reach in just a day
> let alone within the hour you can spare

all right, no flight tonight
tomorrow — back to yesterday

> "Do you want a round trip ticket, sir?"

> "No. I'm just going one way"

California Squares and Sextiles

look back again

to San Francisco's cable cars, climbing flowered paths

        to Hollywood and Vine . . . Big Sur and Tiny Tim
        the Christmas one, with crutches
        and the one who tiptoed
        through television's tulips, with Miss Vicky

look back

beyond the foaming, troubled surf
to where you left your heart
along the winding roads that lead from Carmel to Nepenthe
look back to pine trees, reaching up toward tomorrow
and those with palm leaves drooping in the smoggy air
near MGM and Paramount

        it's not too late

look back

at Jaguars speeding past the dreamers
sipping lemon cokes at Schwab's
a lone, white cross planted on Mount Olympus
against the far hill
behind Grauman's Chinese Theatre
and the signatures of gods and goddesses
graven in cement, below

look back once more

at the golden stretch of beach called Malibu
where Jess Stearn writes away the hours
haunted, maybe
by the echoes of a sleeping prophet

Sunset Boulevard at sunrise
blurring streaks of colored neon on the Strip
waving in zigzag patterns through slanting veils of rain

the train, at L.A. depot
spilling passengers afraid to fly

listen to the throbbing "Sounds of Silence"
and the whimpering cry of Rosemary's baby

clap your hands for Tinker Bell
and sigh for Peter Pan
frolicking among the dancing fountains
and jungle blooms
of the Beverly Hills Hotel

stop beside the gateway guarding garish Forest Lawn
long enough to wonder what twilight has to say
that she should linger on this way

look back

at lonesome cowboys and girls in scarlet tights
swinging on a high trapeze with bearded Lancelots
and barefoot priests of fantasy
from the other side of the grass
— where it may be greener
as Marlon Brando and George C. Scott
challenge the gold-plated Oscar
to a *Duel in the Sun*

look back again
at the uneasy ground where San Andreas lies at fault

      but blameless

driven near to breaking by something more than Nature
bombarding every inch of earth around its bed
            ... and what of evil yet unfed?

          it's not too late
    look back

at Woodstock's lavender smoke
winging magical mystery signals to Paul and John and Mark
and others in the endless line of children
walking through the loneliness with lighted candles
chanting "Peace"

crying out against a hundred kinds of hate and greed
    and war

      sending strong, electric waves of love
      to the trembling Pacific shore

my God! you didn't see them?

    they passed right by your door

will someone please tell Hilly Elkins
who thinks those couples prancing around nude
      in *Oh! Calcutta!*
are the last word in throbbing, sensual passion

      that yesterday I saw two people
      sitting across from each other
      in a crowded, noisy coffee shop
      holding eyes and touching hearts
         and knowing
      how soon and how deep
         but waiting
         just a little while longer

in case he ever wants to produce a show about sex?

Mystery of the Serpent Circle, Secret of the Sphinx

" ... and now the people of Assisi and Bettona
and of all the country around about, saw the church
of St. Mary of the Angels, as it were, on fire

The people of Assisi hastened with great speed
to put out the fire, but on arriving
they saw no fire

only Francis and Claire ..
sitting around their humble meal, on the ground
then they knew that what they had seen
was a celestial fire ..."

From .. The Little Flowers of St. Francis

and more they would have seen
had their earth-eyes not been veiled

for Claire had waited fifteen long and barren years
that Francesco might relent, and sup with her
he, having feared such intimacy might cause scandal

yes, had the good citizens of Assisi and Bettona
gazed upon that blessed night
with the Third Eye's deeper wisdom

they might have seen

sky rockets of the future

druids .. stars .. elves

violet woods and shimmering rainbows

had they listened with the inner ear
they might have heard the music of the spheres

angels singing
carols of tomorrow

in the lingering shadow
of Galilee's scarlet-passioned sorrow
and its painful atonement

     with present vows of chastity to suffer

but promises to keep . . of later

Pluto in Cancer, Exploding

you want to take a trip
or at least smoke a little grass
and you need to borrow some bread?

sorry, sweetheart — I would if I could
your credit is good
it's just that I'm low on cash
and the little I've got won't buy any pot
let alone acid or hash
it's really a pity, but I'm strictly "tap city"

don't go — I'll walk with you awhile, if you want me
and show you what it's like to be born and to die
in one moment of time
I mean, like my own kind of hegira

look! just behind your shoulder
there's a tall, thin steeple
drawing a needle shadow to thread all the people

     see the gypsy lady, winking at the clown
     running up the steps where the lions lie stoned
     guarding the library doors?

cars on the left — cars on the right
go-go-go on the green-green light!
STOP! on the color of raspberry jello ...
the sun is so bright, it's kind of like drowning
in brilliant orangy-yellow

     I know a place with quiet cool shade
     where we can walk barefoot
     and chew pine needles
     to make it Christmas

here in the woods, it's dark and deep
like sleep
we can whisper
and no one can see us or hear us
but God
and He's smiling

       now come over here
       lie down — touch me — feel the grass
       it's green and wet and new
       no, not with dew ... can't you see?
       those sparkling drops are diamonds
       and part of the wet is you and me

your eyes are bursting with colors
and twinkling lights and star shine
they're reflecting the Queen Anne's lace by the pool
       and speaking of royalty

do you know you remind me so ... of King Arthur?
there's still the faintest scar on your forehead
from the wound when you were searching for the Holy Grail

       but listen

do you hear all that love pouring out of the sky
like music?
what a glorious, bell-ringing sound!
it could really blow your mind
whipping in and out of the breeze that's tangling your hair

       hey, doesn't the air
       smell like vanilla?

it's such a fiercely gorgeous high
are you sure you want to smother it?

Capricorn Calendar

how old am I?
I'll be 92 next Christmas
though I won't admit to one day over 20

even after all the birthday cards
are cut and shuffled
it's hard to figure

I've aged at least 500 years
since I stumbled into you
yet I still believe in fairy tales
like "The Princess and the Frog"
    perhaps I'm really only 3 or so?

you'll never know how old I am
but I'll tell you anyway
I was born the hour we met
and died today

Three French Hens — Two Turtle Doves

November and December
are unreal in California

> who can conjure cranberries, or jingle jolly holly
> in such an alien atmosphere?
> only those born here
> who do not have different memories

to these, perhaps, the quiet beauty
of graceful gulls, riding crested waves of snow-capped clouds
in a sea of rosy sky, tinted by the Sunrise glow
high above the Moon-tugged ocean's tides
of emerald ebb and flow
compensates for missing happy winter sleigh rides
over the hills, and through the woods
to grandma's house for hot mince pie and merry mistletoe

who can celebrate Thanksgiving
in a land awash with painted Indians
but short on Pilgrims . . . making Progress?

not lacking hordes of naked savages
worshipping the Sun god
and trading strands of colored beads . . .
but with hardly a practicing Puritan in sight
especially at night
along the gaudy, neon-lighted
hard-core porno Strip
where any vision of a New World ship
is blurred by the swarming pestilence of motorcycles
bearing down on helpless, screaming dunes
leaving trails of noxious fumes, and belching
noisy backfires

not that I miss the Puritans all that much
I never really knew one ..

      but I used to like to draw them
      in their stiff, white collars and tall, buckled hats
      cutting them out in sillouette
      or painting them in water colors, hands folded
                                    praying

      thanking God for Nature's blessings
      before they feasted

      somehow I just can't fool myself
      into imaging Big Sur as Plymouth Rock
      not even when Nepenthe
      has pumpkin pie and turkey on the menu

      the most exotic blooms
      which still survive in Beverly Hills
      and creep their vines around the swimming pools
      of Los Angeles hotels, in the City of Lost Angels
      do not bear much resemblance
      to glittering tree balls, etched with elves

      and palms, of course .. even those not brown from smog
      make unsatisfactory trimmings
      nor did I ever see one masquerading as a Yuletide log
      burning brightly, crackling cheer
                        out here

      it's hard to catch a glimpse of prancing reindeer
      on the twisting L.A. Freeway
                teeming into Mulholland Drive

      O! who can hear the clear and joyous ring

              of a Noel bell

in the balmy air
of the bored, half-hearted spring
Californians manufacture out of winter wishes
to make their oranges grow?

                    .. not even any snow

let alone a William Brewster

or a partridge in a pear tree

Sting of the Scorpion

your icy voice put out the stars
it cracked my heart and broke it in splinters
your tone as cold as Siberian winters

      but I promise to soon forget
      the contract we almost made
      you'll feel the swift response of an equal
      as the dream begins to fade

I'll drown you in pseudo-kindness
and a casual, friendly glance
I can almost imagine your blindness
      as I watch and wait for the chance
      to suddenly — cruelly — make you know
      how easy it was to let you go

Flashback to the Starship Ra-Ram

that startled moment
when we first met

    it was inexplicably silent between us
    though not awkward or uncomfortable in any way
       just a strange oasis of silence
    in a shimmering bubble of reality-illusion
    made from the Babylon sounds of people-confusion

    and we stood in the center of this bubble
    where it was still . . and calm . . and clear
    portending some immense energy and unleashed power
    unseen, unheard . . but felt

            "let those who have eyes see
            let those who have ears hear"

    suspended in a peace that passed all understanding
    like watching the Hopi's weary
                grief-stained Snow Kachina
    wander, at last, into restful haven
    at the appointed hour for the coded birth
    of Vulcan, Mercury and Horus . . yes
                 there were three

    or like standing motionless at the haunted midnight hour
    in the whispering shadow of the Great Pyramid of Giza
    beneath a bereaved and weeping Egyptian Full Moon

        knowing well we dare not tell
        or speak of what we knew
        in words or letters, prose or rhyme
        until the allotted time
            . . which draws ever nearer

do all lovers feel it approaching?
have they read the wise in each other's eyes?
our knowing and theirs .. is different
as chords of music and shades of spectrum vary

but the time draws nearer

      when the Sunset lie
      which has long lain buried
      will be resurrected by Sunrise
      and transfigured into Truth

Echoes from an Earthquaked Temenos

down, down, down

    through countless centuries of tortured time
    beginning ages before the oblivion of Poseidon

    Satan has seeded spiritual slanders
    seething with sinister and serpentine intent
    to mesmerize the subconscious minds of students
    engrossed in the murky myths of Egyptology

    and so these blinded hieroglyphic hierophants
    thus innocently corrupted
    these learned men and women of worldly fame
    having been seduced by the Prince of Death and Darkness

    teach us that the ancient legends claim
    the fair young Horus did swear a cold revenge
    upon the murderer of his father
    a vile oath to return evil for evil
    therefore engaging his uncle, Set
                    in hideous battle

    urged on by his bereaved and bitter mother

                        Isis

    goaded in restless dreams
    by the angry astral of his brave sire

                       Osiris

lies ! lies ! lies !

        can you not hear the outraged cries
        of Cassotis and Cassandra
        from the broken rocks and buried ruins
        of a million adyta ?

    neither trust the perfumed and jeweled wench

                  Nephthys

        for her sisterly devotion was a mask
        hiding sins horrible beyond all earthly measure
        she, who first mated with animals for sensual pleasure
        her womb the beastly terrarium
        of a half-jackal child of Hades called Anubis

no ! no ! no !

        oh ! gullible sheep
        the Truth is not as misguided seers
        have repeatedly told

it happened thus . .

        while Horus fell into a trancelike sleep
        during secret rites in a Temple of old
                at the age of twelve
        Set, cleverly disguised as a Coptic Priest
        did hypnotically induce in the kind, gentle lad
        a thirst for bloody revenge

        as part of a heinous, hellish plan
        to disgrace the grace of Isis and Osiris
        gradually discrediting the memory of Wisdom
        taught by these two, who were *not* twin siblings
        but who were Twin Souls
        whose mission was only to channel the rays

            of Pax et Bonum

true, Isis wept bitter tears
in unimaginable, inconsolable grief
at the awful dismemberment of her mate
by his jealousy-driven, greed-crazed brother

                          Set

yet she knew no hate
and did not drive her son to kill
for she was then — and she is still
as she shall be eternally

              a vessel for Love and Forgiveness

nor was Osiris a retaliatory god
of barbaric custom
destined to rule those icy nether regions
as Judge of the Quick and Dead
for he was then — and he is still
as he shall be eternally

              a vessel for Mercy Everlasting

Who Announces a Saviour?

bearing gifts, they came by camel
following yonder star
to seek the humble one, smelling sweetly of hay
who would herald the Age of the Fish
by touching a few hearts with love and gentle

                    before they nailed him

where are the Wise Men now?
following which star .. and whither?
even the Vatican has redesigned the Catholic prayers
to now label the Wise Men ... the three "astrologers"

                    .. it's never too late for truth
                    to shed its light upon the darkness
                                        of distortion

    but ..

where are the wise astrologers, where?
it's the Aquarian Age, and we're entitled too
we have a right to our own messiah
after all, we've waited roughly two thousand years

                    seems like four or more

and the shepherds on bended knee, where are they?
keeping watch over their flocks by night, I guess
                    flocks of cattle
keeping them safe and warm and plump
till they're slaughtered for the likes of McDonald's
                            or the Steak and Brew

where are the Essenes?

        .. or *were* they, ever?

as for him, the humble one
smelling sweetly of hay
he'd never draw a second glance today
if he once more chose a prostitute to wash his feet
and tenderly smooth his hair

who can tell the prostitutes from the Sweet Sixteens
trying to imitate *Playboy, Playgirl*
Penthouse and *Hustler's* glossy pages of lewdness?

at least *she* was sorry

      for her fault, her fault
      her most grievous fault .... are they?

  "sorry for what?"
  they'd say

        who announces a saviour?

and what is worth saving?
our polluted streams and woods .. and minds?

even the children are rated "X"
yes, suffer the Little Ones to come ..
           and forbid them not

they're predicting kids will be having sex
at the age of ten, by the end of the century

        ... they didn't mention love

my god! that's only twenty years away

government reeks of lust and greed
without a trace of redemptive contrition
as TV commercials blatantly, unblushingly

    openly and obscenely

36

knock the competition by name .. for shame

mugging, drugging, bugging, child abuse
is there any use
to wait ...

   to scan the evening skies for his Morning Star
   suffocated by the sulphurous stench of hate
   and blinded by the smog of selfishness?

perhaps corruption is the millennial manure
that fertilizes messianic music
the winter prelude to *his* springtime song

                    then hurry, Spring ... hurry!

we need your fragrant lavender blossoms
your electrical storms, to clear the air

your sweet, damp grass and hay

                    to smell

so we can pretend a little longer

                    that Hell

      is somewhere else

Funeral of the Flowers

For Mike

*in defense of Moe, the Pearls
and all their friends*

by what insane and twisted logic
do they label grafitti on the subway cars
                    vandalism ?

            can they not see that much of it
            is Zeus-inspired . . . . .

                                        angel-instigated ?

            a fresh rainbow of hope, splashed on dreary
            speeding streaks of oblong steely ugliness

                                        going nowhere
            save perhaps to hell

                    on a rising fare

            they should offer weekly wages
            an occasional bronze cast medal, maybe
            as a gesture of gratitude
            to those joyous, free-spirited artists
            immortalized by Norman Mailer
            who miraclize Manhattan's misery

                            with their magic mantras

            instead, the Rapid Transit Authorities
            in filthy Fun City
            have found a tough new paint for their coffins

glum, gun-metal grey, to match their souls

totally resistant to colors
flowers, butterflies and sunny verses

not comprehending
that the messages of Aquarian prophets
rang out wistful warnings
                    from their subway walls and cars

preferring burial to resurrection
                    as they dim the bright reflection

of tomorrow's wishing stars

leaving only lonely echoes
of the lyrical sounds of children's laughter
and the subtle Uranian wisdom offered

                    by youthful Masters Of Eternity
                    symbolized by M.O.E.

blind beasts of Babylon

blotting out the beauty of grafitti
but leaving on display for us, untouched

                    the obscene art exhibit

of Deep Throat posters .. "snuff" and cannibalism films

                    newsstands smeared

with Playgirls masturbating on the covers

and the porno parlors blighting Broadway's

                    fading lights

And the Angel Said: "Fear Not"

you intruded upon my solitude
like some uninvited visitor in the silent night
O! holy night

how did you get past the Watch Dogs at the gate
and the sign that plainly said: KEEP OUT?

I had run in off the darkened, teeming streets
of Los Angeles, City of Angels — fallen
to escape the recorded "Ave Marias"
pouring from public speakers
blended with the steady tolling of Salvation Army bells

.. "Sister, can you spare a quarter or a dime?"

accompanied by a clear soprano reminder
of another lonely, waiting street
in another darkened time ..

"O! little town of Bethlehem
how still we see thee lie
above thy deep and dreamless sleep
the silent stars go by
yet in thy dark streets shineth
an everlasting light
the hopes and fears of all the years
are met in thee tonight .."

blinking back an unexpected mist of tears
that rose up from an inner well of sorrow, seeking haven
I rushed quickly through the nearest open doorway

and suddenly ... you were standing there

a tall, wise man

sending me a gentle smile
across the narrow, crowded aisle
                        of Pickwick Bookstore

unlikely cradle for a miracle
why not the Madonna Inn
where we went months later
and were told they had "no room"?

for a spinning moment

I thought you had materialized
from another planet or star
        a familiar stranger

gazing calmly through the stained glass windows
                                of my eyes

stained with memories of recent grief
and the gathered dust .. of old mistrust

I returned your smile, uncertain
while with some mystical permission
surely not from me
you rang the bells of my heart, long stilled
knocked on the door of my mind, till it opened

then reverently, as monks walk
you entered the dark and lonely temple of my soul

        to light a candle

"it's going to snow tonight
I feel it in the air .."

do you see how white the Pyramid gleams
by moonlight over there?

"I thought it never snowed
in California .."

the music of the Nile is crashing
in my ear .. do you not hear?

"it doesn't very often
but I believe it will this year ..
maybe we could make some snowflakes fall
if we concentrated hard"

bringing in the logs
for the long, cold winter
promises of later, far away

"you mean, if we pray?"

"yes .. miracles can happen
if you really want them too"

silver ships and rolling thunder
déjà vu .. oh, déjà vu!

"well, I don't know .."

"you mean you've never made it snow
just by wishing it so?"

"that sort of magic
is only possible in a dream"

       beating tom-toms, smoky campfires
       wild bird's scream

              "I'll prove it to you!
              then we'll make some snow ice cream
              it's healthier than the kind
              that's made with sugar"

"yes, I guess that's true"

       oh, the Nile is blue, so blue

              "say, do you read Charlie Brown?
              do you believe in astral projection?
              and are you against the A.M.A.?"

"yes I do! I mean, yes, I am!
also the F.D.A."

       even Pharaohs turn to clay

              "now I *know* I'm right!
              it *will* snow tonight"

"yes, I suppose it might
if we really pray .."

43

August 31, 1971: 11:29 P.M.

maybe Raphael's and Botticelli's jeweled colors
Rembrandt's and Da Vinci's too .. were real

            not just painted

the way life looks
through crystals of tenderness

                you smiled at me tonight
                at the bottom of the stairs
                with so much love in your eyes
                swimming in a mist
                            of almost-tears

                all you said was

            "let's go for a walk in the woods
            tomorrow, at dawn
                    just you and me, alone
            before the world's awake

            I'll show you
            how we can make a deer come near
            by remaining very, very still
                    ... projecting kindness"

and all I said was

"I'll set the alarm for five"

            but we were stained glass
            ruby red and azure blue
            and the choir was singing

Ring the Bells and Tell the People!

oh, the miracle of us!

      at last we found a mountain who could fly
      a mountain who could soar across the sky
      and flap its feathered peaks
                      like some giant snow bird
      dipping in and out of clouds

      when you and I were watching it together
      with trembling hands and singing hearts
      rubbing noses, making magic .. then

                how it flew!

      showing off the acrobatics it had learned to do
      all through the centuries of waiting for our Faith

      yes, at last we found a mountain who could fly

           Pike's Peak, in Colorado

      sometimes it wore, our mountain,
      silver streaks of starlight in its hair, at dusk
      or at sunset, trailing rosy ribbons

      sometimes the shimmering, lemon-sliced New Moon
      painted it with lavender at dawn
      and not to be outdone in this
      the yellow round balloon Full Moon
      would brush it with a kiss of midnight blues

      then, jealous of seduction's softer hues
      the brilliant red-orange Sun, at noon
      blazed it in pink-gold splashes
      drenching its snow-capped peaks with dazzling white

oh! there were never shadows cast upon it
day or night
by either luminary

for shadowed mountains only cry
and cannot fly

how could shadows ever fall
on such a magic mountain?

it was too wild and beautiful
looming there so proud and high
against a robin's-egg-blue sky

and smiling down

upon the teeny-tiny, cobweb
ghost-filled, gold mining town
called Cripple Creek

nor could storm clouds ever gather
above our funny crooked house
on a little crooked street
in that happy, teeny-tiny, cobweb
slipping-off-the-time-track town

snuggled safely in the loving arms
of our flying mountain
who cradled it tenderly for us
and sang to it each night
a haunting lullaby of déjà vu

.. without a name

until we came

and flew unto
our happiness

we flew in your dusty blue and winging Bug
    through puffs of snowball clouds
and laughing skies
      to the sound of musical butterflies
up winding roads
      past the deep-deep-deep-cool-green
      of murmuring pine and hemlock woods
slowing down
    then bending low, to flow
          beneath the Tunnel of Time
and passing through it, both could see
                Forever

    clearly
      looming
just ahead of us

    so how could there be

      shadows?

Stonehenge Caper

do you know what it is about us
that brings my deepest serenity
my most trembling springs
and the clearest rings of the silver bells
in my heart?

it's that small funny druid thing
we do with each other
when I'm baking biscuits or taking a bath
changing a typewriter ribbon
feeding the kittens, or brushing my hair

and you're reading e. e. cummings
cleaning out the fireplace
melting wax for Christmas candles
or standing on your head
near the dining-room chair

and our eyes meet .. to lock
in a deep, deep knowing

then we fly together

touch noses

and whisper

"magic"!

And the Warm of Him

                    there are lots of things
                    I couldn't talk about
                            while I was waiting

fat and dimpled pink-smelling babies
clinging to my skirts
while I baked golden loaves of bread
and maybe even churned the butter
clear cool water drawn from the well
in wooden buckets .. clean fresh winds
whipping the clouds of a storm

            and the warm of him

                    bringing in the logs
                            for the long cold winter
                    and making me tremble
                    with the promise in his eyes
                                .. of later

            there were lots of things
            I couldn't talk about
                    while I was waiting

walking barefoot through silent woods
stars glittering in the branches
of tall fir trees .. soft green moss
dark brown eyes piercing mine
bride red feathers .. turquoise beads
smokey prayers around the campfire
my fine white horse
swifter than the north wind

strong handsome Brave
and favorite of the Sun God
sweet hot breath against my breast
lips murmuring .. arms clinging
blood churning
loins burning .. while the rain
beat gentle on the tent
near the lake
and the pale Moon faded into dawn
at the moment
when the wild birds cry

there are so many things
I never told
while I was waiting

silver ships with swelling sails
the music of the Nile .. crashing chords of glory
emerald serpent with ruby eyes
Pharaoh's tomb .. Egyptian skies

and the warm of him

lying naked dead beside me
in the shadow of the Pyramid
gleaming white
in the Moon's pale light
buried secrets in desert sands
myrrh scented skin
familiar hands
and O! the Nile is blue .. so blue

there are lots of things
I kept inside
.. while I was waiting

brass gongs ringing through the hills
oceans rolling thunder .. nights full of wonder
hot humid breezes blowing over beaches
wet eyes shining ..... catching sunbeams

and the warm of him

teaching me to match
the rhythm of the sea gulls
move and sway back and forth
move together back and forth
explode in fire!
then cool green water
floating .. floating .. explode in fire!
cool green water
again and again
and again

misty fogs on Scottish bogs
Irish meadows starred with shamrocks
rocking softly as voices keen

Kathleen, Kathleen

I'll take you home ..

the White Cliffs of Wales
kissed by Sun and foam
three infants' faces

fine white laces

satin breeches, golden crown
                London Towers, falling down
        so many walks near Notre Dame

    déjà vu

                oh, déjà vu . . . !

    so many things I never told

                and then you came . . and you knew

Alice's Hexagram

in the beginning
I used to puzzle myself
about what was missing from our Wonderland

> ... certainly not the Red Queen or the Mad Hatter
> it was only yesterday that we had tea with *them* ...

and after I knew what it was
our moments together were smudged with restlessness

> but now I sit near you
> quietly content
> and deeply peaceful
> gazing through the looking glass
> of a car, a bus, a plane or a train
> paying no attention at all to the White Rabbit
> and his threatening pocket watch
> nor to the second hand

for I Ching says:

> when the clouds grow heavy with moisture
> one only has to wait
> the rain will surely come
> ten pairs of tortoises cannot prevent it
> and perseverance furthers

The Very First Time

I'm glad you awakened the overflowing wells of love in me
for the first time ever

                          in the sunlight

so I could see your smile of awe and pride
and you could see the tremor of my wonderment
at this unsuspected secret
I never knew that I contained

                   within my waiting body

waiting lonely .. only for your touch
to trust you with my mysteries of being woman

          now I feel like a stream

yes, now I know how a stream feels
rushing out to meet the river
           that draws it on .. and on .. and on
into the ocean

             then into final oneness
             with the Universe

our lovemaking . .

is like a flaming volcano of mysterious origin
lightning flashes at its summit
                and quaking at its base
rain falling in its hollows
       with hot lava pouring over us
in an uncontrollable avalanche

then swirling into baby rivers
                   of tenderness
      and gentle

an alternating stream
           anew each time
and new and new
       that flows into
and calms and steadies . . our souls

Knowing

will I ever solve the twin-riddled mystery
of our knowing — and of us?

>   the knowing-things we shared
>   when we first stared, so deeply
>   into each other's eyes
>   we've never spoken of again

>   though we've discussed related matters
>   like serpent circles, quarks and angstrom units
>   the body and the brain, death and birth
>   and other secrets of Heaven and Earth

>   but not the staring and staring of our sharing
>   the flowing energy, glowing eyes
>   and the surprise of our trancelike speech

>   so silvery-wise

>   now, each time the staring
>   and the growing-knowing returns
>   through that pulsing force that burns
>   we are silent, transfixed
>   within the vortex of our strange tornado

>   of knowingness

>   by some unspoken galactic agreement
>   not feeling the necessity to utter a syllable
>   the eyes into eyes, like lasar embers
>   are enough

>   we have not again needed words
>   when our pyramidic moments come and go
>   always suddenly, unexpectedly

for no reason, in the middle of a sentence
we stop
        and stare
            and *know* . . . . .

in silence

until gradually they've become, our moments
a coming and a going thing
                an unspeakable knowing-thing
a time when we learn so much

yet, I can never recall a single searing thought
passed along the silver-blue cord connecting us
when it's over .. like waking
                    from a dream

I long to ask if you consciously remember
the wisdom so strangely implanted
by our eternity ember's communion
but your eyes forbid verbal inquiry

and so my questions remain unanswered
sometimes burning inside me, in the night
lying beside you, warm and near
the silent knowing-thing between us

like a deeper spring, remembered

            yet forgotten

A Sign to Remind Me

I left my home of rough green wood
a blue velvet couch

I dream till now

a shiny dark bush
just left of the door

down the walk
clickity clacks
as my doll in her carriage
went over the cracks

"we'll go far away"

.. Marilyn Monroe

a six year old with rosy cheeks
                  and pigtails tied with yellow yarn
is skipping rope in front of me

she plays each day I walk near Central Park
like a sign of teeny-tiny to remind me

oh! she expects a miracle
every hour or so .. and finds it
sometimes it's a perfectly marvelous flower
being kissed by a bumble bee
or a lady bug, who has landed gently
                          on her knee

and who must be set free
with the magical mantra of "lady bug, lady bug
                        fly away home!"

so she won't lose her way
and forget .. where she lives

58

yesterday, she found the green miracle
of a grasshopper
and watched it hop over the cracks
                              in the sidewalk
for hours

then tried to coax it to hop back into the grass
in the park .. a block away

                    before it, too, was lost

          I think it was she
          who did that
          or maybe it was me

when I'm pretending I'm small enough
to play with bugs and birds and things
and believe in shiny gold wishing rings
that get lost — then found
and hear the sound
of a robin .. before he sings

and have twin lady bugs land
on each of my knees

              to talk with me awhile

before they fly away

Question for Norma Jean

the whole world is aware of every detail
of your War Years
you fought those battles bravely
                          painfully and slow

keeping well hidden your membership
in God's own Secret Service .. and earned
your purple heart
under the false identities of Baker .. and Monroe

                    thanks to the lies
                    woven and recorded
                          by poor, childless Gladys

it's your Prairie Years they need to know
those years from which they all

                    can learn so much

those years of secrets, buried
nearly a century before your star-crossed birth
upon this ever-growing-more-insensitive

                          planet Earth

Norman Mailer dutifully and duly noted
that your bedroom walls were once devotedly covered
with pictures of the tall and lanky one

                    who wept at Gettysburg

is that why you fell so helplessly in love
with Joe and Arthur and Yves
three who, each in his own way, were called

                          "Lincolnesque"
in stature, mannerisms
                    or gentleness of heart?

did you sense that Jim Dougherty
and Bob Slatzer also possessed a haunting part
of Honest Abe's integrity?

and is that why you were Ram-determined
to meet your other idol, Sandburg .. Carl?

then, when the two of you were at last
together briefly, among the fragile mountain laurel
of his country home
                laughing delightedly, like children
to find so many joys in common
not the least of these your mutual poetry of soul

did your Higher Selves perchance discuss
the deeper mystery
that you may have been .. five times a twin

                        and also kin

to him, whom Sandburg
well loved and long respected?

for Sandburg sadly, quietly knew the secret
of the small, pathetic little girl called Ella
standing on a chair in Springfield
as the lanky lawyer softly murmured

                ".. see? you're not as tall
                        as I am .. even now"

yes, Sandburg knew — he knew

but did he also know
of the birthright given by that child

                to you?

April Prophecy: Southern Cross of Northern Lights

don't cry, my doll
don't cry
I hold you and rock you to sleep

hush, hush! I'm pretending now
I'm not your mother who died

                      .. Marilyn Monroe

on an unexpected windswept day in April
I listened to a priest of God pay timid tribute
to a defenseless and once fabled legend

            "Thy servant, Howard"

frail eulogy, lasting barely seven minutes
leaving one to wonder
if this soul's only earthly contribution
had been accumulating wealth
                    while shod in tennis shoes

sterile service, deigning to remind us
that the genius known as Howard Robard Hughes
had entered this world with nothing
and surely could take nothing from it with him now

drab, somber ritual of Lent
never questioning
whether such had even been the man's intent

how many millions watched with me
the flickering Texas shadows
of that starkly frigid Houston homage to the dead?
like guilty secrets
        creeping craven past the TV screen

                    .. no tears were shed, they said

perhaps they didn't notice mine

        did he ?

my heart kept eldritch tempo to an inner dirge in minor key
as I stared at sixteen grim, stone chiseled figures
one inappropriately named "Gay"
gathered in gloom around a casket, closed over
                                    whose remains ?

mute, metal box, so stern, so real
like a collier, bearing coals
                to charred Newcastle's harbor
no mourners, these, but uninvited strangers here
and I felt a sudden sense of surging loss

                        could it be true
                        that no one shed
                        a single tear .. ?

except for her, who may have wept inside
to dampen quinine bitter memories
while she held still her tongue and high her head

            .. he was her sister's boy

            or so they said

now laid to rest in a lonely, unmarked grave
did she once kiss him on the cheek
                when she tucked him into bed ?

my wrists grew trembling, limp and weak
while a warning prelude pulse
                spread throughout my veins
portending a transfusion of terror
                pounding steady, slow

as I felt the presence of a ghost I never met
                        nor cared to know
yet did not try to chase away
            wishing almost he would stay
to keep me Saturn-shy and cobweb company

how many miles, I asked him, from Florida to Vancouver
or from Nome to London Town, via Mexico and Dallas?
it must be more than fourscore miles and ten
could I go there by candlelight?

                then came his quiet answer, calm

                "yes, and back again"

I've often heard it told, I murmured to him low
that winter's sealed with ice in Anchorage, Alaska
yet the frozen heart, they say, is ever thawed
in its cryogenic hope of a warmer summer Sun,
this hinted by the Northern Lights
spectrum-streaked with shades of green and gold
overlaid with lavender's reds and blues

could such a rainbow also someday thaw
the frozen, silent mystery of a man called Howard Hughes?

                "the mystery of which Hughes?"

                my ghostly friend inquired

            "daredevil aviator
                    financial wizard
            restless dreamer
                    enigmatic genius

            or eccentric recluse, old and weary
            whom some called mad?"

were there then, so many men
called Howard Hughes?
each sailing on a haunted Star Quest
to some strange, predestined shore?

and while I wondered, suddenly it thundered
as if to punctuate his angry answer

> *"there once were four*
> *now minus three*
> *and leaving one"*

my ghost was speaking in twin riddles

       yes, twin . . riddles

or did he speak a sibling code of retribution
fragmented prisms, but dimly glimpsed, and darkly
through a shattered mirror of the past
reflecting back earthquaking secrets, long untold?

    eccentric recluse
         weary and old
   whom some have
       called insane?

a faint, unspeakable horror
sought to nearly surgically implant itself

           . . *within whose brain?*

as my thoughts were shrouded
in a shapeless cloud of rising dread

      is Howard Hughes not dead?

or does the man, not just the legend
            perchance live still
unknown to those
who have so long abused and used his name

                    misread his "will"?

but all I heard, in veiled, bereaved reply
was an echo, like a sigh, spinning in a tomb

                              "four minus three
                               now leaving one"

          vibrating in the room

till I was blinded by a bursting Midnight Sun
and astrally transported to a far and unfamiliar place
where I thought I stood beside a shadow
               with a kind, yet etched-with-sorrow face

the shadow of a man grown sure and Lincoln tall
hidden by the brilliance of the Northern Borealis light
as the night grew bright with recognition

then dreamt I heard a whisper

                    from the frozen sounds of silence
                    in Anchorage, Alaska

borne upon an icy wind
invigorating, fresh and clean .. alive

                    "I shall return to tell the truth
                     before the towers of Babylon have fallen"

Lecture to a Lion Tuned In to Uranus

now, see here — you can't just go around
expecting everybody to be concerned
about the dangers of acid rain
and the disappearance of plankton

    or thinking that everyone understands
why Henry Miller paints sweet and sour, like he writes
        (because maybe he lived in the Orient
        in a former life)

not everyone has heard about Edgar Cayce and his trances
or Cleve Backster's polygraphs and plants

sometimes you have to come down from the lighthouse
and play with the sandpipers
    skipping and staggering on the beach
if you want them to eat the crumbs of eternity
you've stored up to feed them
now that winter is coming to the world

my God, some people still go to Roseland Ballroom
and dance all night
to "One O'Clock Jump" and "Stella By Starlight"

    or save up for one of those group vacations in Hawaii
    and bring home color Polaroids
    of hula girls hanging leis around their necks

or wander through the strobes of Studio 54
wearing their Sony deaf-proof earplugs
and blinking in the simulated rainbows

    or wait in line outside
    for hours
    to get Margaux Hemingway's autograph

Premature Götterdämmerung

I have pondered long and sadly
what you said
about the certain, tragic future just ahead
for a waning planet, drenched in murky, poisoned air
infected by polluted oceans, swollen with rancid refuse
nature's cool green velvet quilts
ripped and ruined

land laid waste and ravaged
bleeding from the rape of greedy gorging
stripped naked of its nourishment
by blind and selfish plunder
haunted by the shrieks of murdered baby seals
and the ghosts of butchered leopards

soaked through with the stench of sure decay
the final gasp so near
it must be measured by the year
instead of by the century

and so, you say, you will not bring a child
into a world so soon to be expired

I've shuddered at the harsh statistics of despair
which could allow this sterile judgment
to find roots in such as you
whose tears reflect the memory of angels running free
through fields streaked yellow by the morning sun
whose ears still hear the carols of their laughter

and, as always
I have rushed to walk beside you on your way to truth
to try to see it clearly through your eyes

you paint a picture of a lovely, pulsing ball
within our solar system
profanely debauched by amoral brutes
who have used it shamefully, for pleasure
and torn its flesh
with repeated, painful nuclear thrust
to father grotesque mutation

who have bruised its fragile beauty
leaving it to die
like a frail, emaciated body
pale and wan
while they lie drunk and babbling senseless songs
"Diddle Diddle Dumpling, My Son John"
going — going — very soon gone
slain in careless orgy
just before the dawn
of Hell

and now I feel with you excruciating sorrow
and share your angry, urgent need
to halt this mad and ruthless blasphemy
that threatens man and beast and fish and fowl

we can, we shall, we must
pull back these lengthening shadows from our Sun
and mobilize each outraged soul
to strike a furious blow for life
            today
before tomorrow's lost in dust
don't stop to count the cost in time or coin
when it may be too late
before another dozen Springs of ours
            or theirs
have passed

but wait —
listen to the soft, permissive sighing
as erotic lullabies of doom
crooned to lazy, silken melodies
are amplified through spinning, electronic discs
and whirls of flashing, colored lights

look closely in the burning face of evil

unholy masquerader —
who is that
who gazes back into our eyes
with smile so bright
his hair so fair and golden?

who is that
who sits so tall behind the wheel
to press the gas
and vomit fumes of filth into already sickly air?
who dares to multiply himself into a hundred thousand devils
swinging in a frantic, frenzied dance of death
dumping trash in the streams of Michigan
to keep Ohio clean?

burst a bag of shiny dreams
see how white the toothpaste gleams?
break it, smash it, spit out cans, stain the sands

who dares explode hydrogen hate
deep inside the bowels of earth
stirring sleeping giants
to stretch awake beneath the soil, unseen?

who hides behind screaming banners of progress
bulldozing flowered meadows, slashing trees

clubbing wildlife, grabbing pasture, faster — faster
plaster billboards, spread cement
for countless millions of polished beetles
blasting down the midnight roads
groaning under loads of drugged and singing
saints of sin?

who dares excite the fire that lights the fuse
on the time bomb of a billion random seeds
sprung from the sensual loins of lust
adding wanton procreation to destruction?

who is curious, yellow, for topless, bottomless, mindless sex?
are not insane, lewd scenes of human violation
as much a crime
as those against *her* pure and spacious skies?
she, remember, also once a virgin
proud of purple mountain majesties
and amber waves of grain

look fierce into the face of evil
see how he wears a crown of crimson roses on his head
to greet the newly wed
and nearly dead
on their journey into Nothing

how dare he imitate your blameless, honest features?
how dare he call with carefree voice to sound like mine?

look hard into the glittering eyes of evil
be sure you see

     his face is you — his face is me

belching blindly in the market place

call the vile and vicious stranger in our midst
by his rightful name, with shame

                    for only then
will Truth come crashing through the constellations
              in time to turn the tide
                  and only then
can we make fresh clean winds blow once again
across the snowy mountain tops
                  of this dying earth

                  and only then
deserve to hear his waiting, newborn cry
wrapped in the gentle blankets of our longing
                  and our love

Merry Christmas, Everyone and God Bless Tiny Tim

our first morning of waking together
is etched upon my heart
like a fine steel engraving of a Currier and Ives print

> I awoke to see the pale December solar rays
> painting little pastel splashes
> of dancing rainbow patches on the carpet

> in the town of saints

>> St. Mary's, West Virginia, where we first awoke
>> together, so many years ago?

> or the City of Lost Angels

>> Los Angeles, California, where we found
>> each other .. again?

> no matter

I was back within the sleep-warm, protective circle
of your arms once more
watching the fingers of light streaming across the bed
bathing your familiar features in gentle pink-gold ...
coaxing your eyelids to blink open

and I snuggled near you
in a surge of peace and joy, so strangely blended
squeezing my eyes to keep back the tears
as a great welling up of thanksgiving spread inside me
and nearly burst into music

> ... then you stirred

> *"darling, good morning"*

"good morning, darling"

Half a Pound of Peppermint Tea

... memories of 1970
at Year's End ...

on the morning of our third day

when you were sudsing yourself with lathers of happiness
and I was brushing my hair with happy too
making it crackle with sparks .. I was standing
near the bathroom door

and you stuck your soapy head
around the shower curtain
looked deeply into my eyes .. and smiled

that's all — just smiled

then I loped over to the window
and looked out on the small white cross
planted on Mount Olympus .. on the far hill
behind Grauman's Chinese Theatre
remembering what you had whispered
the night before, after our December spring

"darling, love has made us
a god and goddess"

as I began to croon
a tangled up Mother Goose tune

"oh! this is the day they give miracles away
with half a pound of peppermint tea"

but I never got to tell you what I was singing
there were too many little hurry-bells ringing!

we had to get dressed, and fly outside
to see the world for the very first time
all clean and fresh and bright and shining

and that whole, entire, live-long day
we ran up and down the holly-berry town
                              of Hollywood

giving miracles away
to lonely Scrooges everywhere

then we stopped in C. C. Brown's, across from the Roosevelt
to have some peanut-butter cookies
                    and peppermint tea

served by a jolly lady, with snow-white hair
wearing crinkles and twinkles and smiles
             . . . who was obviously Mrs. Santa Claus
just helping out in the rush hour . . .
and beaming little splashes of joy on us
as we floated around in our cherry-wood booth
                              gazing on each other
like delighted children
dizzied and dazzled by a glittering Christmas tree

          with a Star of Truth at the top

a truth our love had opened up for us to see
for we had found
that the more miracles of happiness
                    we gave away to others

          the more we had left

          for you and me

Abracadabra

you crazy, wonderful, outrageous nut
you're stuck in some kind of mystical rut!

    running around Hollywood, like an overgrown druid
    trying so hard to be teeny-tiny and magical

        . . that's not easy to do
           when you're six foot two

    and thinking you can make miracles
    as effortlessly and swiftly as an elf at the North Pole
    makes a red-and-white-striped peppermint candy cane

        today you even tried to stop the rain

    it was pouring cats and dogs outside

               and you said

          "I'll bet I can bring out the Sun
           for you . . and stop the rain
                  just watch!"

    then you squeezed your eyes tightly
    and concentrated tightly too
            squeezing your mind
    and you prayed and prayed
    and you waited . . and waited . . and waited
    and you believed . . and believed . . and believed

        murmuring, *"Abracadabra . . . magic!"*

oh, you were so grieved
          it hurt you so, I know
when the rain wouldn't stop
you just stood there .. forlornly
in your sloshy Jerusalem sandals
                your toes all squishy-squashy wet
with tiny raindrops sparkling on your lashes

and I watched your yellow-gold aura
grow dimmer around your head, as you said

          softly, so sadly

                "I guess I lost my bet"

no, you didn't stop the cloudburst — you failed
but you tried, you tried, you tried!
that's what was so perfectly marvelous . . .
                . . . you *tried*

do you know how it made me ache inside
and how deeply I understood?

it gave me a sharp loving-pain
when you tried so hard to stop the rain

  and believed so hard that you could

Realization

you are a man who walks in quiet
carefully avoiding waterfalls of words
your feelings run in tranquil streams
flowing surely into the deeper ocean
                              of your passions

there was once a troubled time
when I required your loyalty insured aloud
your devotion spoken constantly, to calm
my restless spirit
and you were patient with my fears

but you are a man wrapped soft in silence
not trusting paragraphs of promises
believing faithfulness is not
                    a verbal thing

and now, at last, I know
your love for me cannot be found in speeches
nor in ballads of eternal declaration

but in the touch of your hand on mine
and the song of longing

                in your quiet eyes

by heart I know the lyric
as a lullaby is memorized in childhood
and hear its melody
each time I submit to your strength

     each time I am conquered

by your gentleness

My Sixth Sense Is You

sometimes, like now ..

    I close my eyes, and let myself sink softly
    into warm-scented pillows of comfort and happy
    drinking in the sounds and smells
    when you are somewhere nearby
    doing fresh and sunny daytime things

I hear you and I smell you

    brushing your teeth with creamy, foaming mint
    splashing in the bath tub, sending out clean soap aromas
    scratching matches across the grate, to light a fire
    that fills the house with the fragrance of woodsmoke
                    and Christmas pine

    making cheerful symphonies of tinkling music
    when you stir your carrot juice
    and strike the spoon against the glass

    or bringing in the morning paper and the mail
    your cheeks smelling like wet snow
        trailing little whiffs of ozone as you walk

my favorite sounds

    are the wild, piercing Tarzan yells you scream in the woods
    when you're bursting with the joy of just being alive
    the funny, froggy noises you make, in bed
    when you're slowly struggling up from sleep

    the trembling tenderness in your voice
    when you whisper "deep" ... our private word of need
    for a sudden, aching hunger that will not wait

my favorite smell

    is your hair in the Sun .. sweet
                              damp
                              and musty
     like a bird's nest

darling ..

let's have our toast and coffee later

       "deep"

Albert Had a Theory

I can't say how .. or why .. or when
but since you and I turned into Us
I know our Now .. was also Then

how many times
have we felt this need?

the Present is but a memory
               we're moving through
at a different rate of speed

the beautiful simplicity
of Einstein's relativity is clear

Yesterday will soon return
and Tomorrow has already been here

now I shall not ever fear to draw
my final Earthbound breath

for there is no Life
until you love
and then there is no death

Pass the Peace Pipe

(THE CAPITULATION OF A CARDINAL FIRE SIGN)

you want to call the shots?
all right, jump on your horse
and I'll walk three respectful steps behind
like a proper squaw

you decide the course and by-ways
our stream of madness shall run
    how it bends and wanders
and where and when it flows
into the land-of-the-singing-waters

I'll chew my moccasins and string my wampum
in the pale, new moon, beside my wickiup
and wait for your bird call, tom-tom beat or smoke puff

but remember, brave Chief Rain-in-the-Heart
while you lead us down this sun-danced warpath
of pride and passion, truth and lie
the spirits of the wind and stars are watching
and it's Manitou who calls the final shots
        not you or I

Mercury Survival Kit

if you ever get caught in a round or two
of the head shrinkers' current favorite game
called "truth confrontation"
prepare yourself for a possible shock
that can lock a heart
or screw a mind uptight

you know the rules
all players sock it to each other like it is
to peel away layers of self-pretense
with no points given
for the desperate maneuvers of self-defense
or strategies to salvage pride
        and when you pass "Go"
        you collect 200 pieces
        of a massive wounded ego

but if you really want to win
and cut straight through all the lies
remember that you don't play "truth" with words
you play it with your eyes

Jupiter Prayer on Christmas Eve

I'm in a panic

      the mistletoe and holly
      are tacked where they ought to be

and the wine is chilled

      but the ghost of Christmas last
      when December turned into a block of solid ice
      between us
      is leering through my shuttered window

you told me it was ghoulish to trim a dead tree
like hanging jewelry on a corpse in the parlor

      ... yours is naked throughout the merry season
      carefully tended in a pot of earth
      later planted outside where it can grow tall ...

this year, mine is bare and potted too
and I give it lots of water

yes, you'll like the tree

      it's the rug

that huge, spreading warmth
of the glossy, satin-brown Iceland Pony
on the floor

      I never thought ...

      what should I do?

I can't hide it in the closet
it's jammed with other things that make you frown
my Frank Sinatra albums, all those ash trays
strings of colored lights and tinsel
and the poems I wrote last winter

>   but I can't just leave it there
>   I don't think I could stand the look on your face
>   when you see that fur
>   and the reflection in your eyes
>   of the pony's pain when he was murdered
>   . . . or did he die a natural death?

never mind, it's still unkind
to have him stretched out on the floor
and walk across his beauty

>   I hope it didn't hurt him—I really do
>   and I hope it didn't hurt the steer you served me once
>   at your house
>   when he was struck in the head with a bloody axe
>   by a butcher singing Noels
>   with no ether

>   or the gentle, brown-eyed cow
>   who gave her life for your shoes

I find I'm crying now
for all of them

>   and I didn't want to cry again this Christmas

>   there's the lobby buzzer
>   you'll be at the door any minute

oh, will you forgive me for the pony?

        I won't walk across him anymore

I guess I know how that is ...
like people you love
when they walk across your heart

        back and forth
        every day
        every night
        and think you have no feelings
        just because you lie there so still

Pluto Moves Slowly but Surely

look, my blueberry sometimes friend

   could I take a raincheck?

I'd like to skip this passing storm
with its violent thunder of knowing
between lightning flashes of guessing
and intermittent torrents of hurt

   we're in that dangerous manic-depressive phase
   of giving each other emotional ink blot tests
     on public couches
   and when one of us makes a Freudian slip
     we switch roles
   like two charming but knife-sharp clever
     diplomats
   each unwilling to commit himself
   for fear of an unexpected coup de grâce

call me when it's time to surrender
my blueberry always love
I think I'll pass this next round
of Russian roulette with words

   it would be just my luck to win

eyes of an arrogant, but gentle stranger
eyes I once knew so well
       why is the night so still?

arms I remember
rainbow that died
       thunder that crashed on a hill

smile of a proud and an intimate stranger
thoughts I can clearly hear
bringing familiar pain
dream half-forgotten ... music that echoes

       why did it start to rain?

"Come on, let's go—don't be so slow"

       did someone say Alsace Lorraine?

"Not me. You'd better hurry if you don't want to miss
       your plane"

November Song

I listen to the drowsy autumn rain
sounding a silver symphony on the old tin roof
as it pitter-patters silver splatters

                              in my brain

but I remain
awake

why am I aloof
to the rain on the roof tonight?
when other times it brings me peace
and the blessed release from awareness

                              called sleep

that sends me out of this world
of illusionary reality
into the world of dreams, and true reality
where the soul is free to fly

              so why do I lie here awake?

somewhere in the musical splatters
of this silvery slumber song
I hear a gong .. and feel the tug
of a silver cord, that once did bind

                      a silvery gong

echoing through the vaulted monasteries
of my mind
from Himalaya's higher altitudes
calling Tibetan monks to pray
from far, far away .. I hear their chants

              this is the world of illusion
              this is the world of illusion

and still the rain
goes pitter-patter in my brain

pitter-patter, what's the matter
silvery sleepy-making melody
pitter-patter, what's the matter

silvery slumber song, what's wrong?
a refrain of pain, pittering and pattering
silvering and splattering
in my brain, this autumn rain

oh, what does it mean?
what does it all mean?

what can I glean from the pitter-patter
from the mystical-crystal-splatter
of this silvery-serpent-seven-heaven-patter
like Judas silver, pounding down upon my head

     rain .. God's own teardrops

but the Judas silver of whose denial
                   whose betrayal?

     his .. or yours .. or mine?

what difference does it make?
you've been gone so long, so long
and all you've left me is a silvery song
to pitter and patter
and splash and splatter ... like tears
streaking down the cheeks of my soul

heal me, silver rain
O! heal this unbearable pain

     of the birth of our Gethsemane

Prelude

our souls are inseparable, forever fused
in some long forgotten heaven

the electrical impulses of our auras
formed through misty eons of time
pulse in rhythm, and create such light
that all who see us say ..

> "what brightness there is around them!
> do they love?"

yes, we love

in each pride and each passion
we are the same
there is only one difference between us

after an unintended hurt
from one of us to the other
I must, I *must* cry out!

for pain infuses me
with a deep, intense urge to talk

and pain fills you
with a deep intense need to walk
in silent gloom inside your room

so close we are
and yet so far apart in this

of what stern stuff is it made
the high forbidding wall that separates us now?
is it made from the glacial ice
of your protective, emotion-locked poise?

or from the rougher bricks
of my jarring noise
and screaming indignation?

no matter

each block of your ice, each brick of my anger
is sealed with the cement of our twin fear
that we are not really, completely loved
each, by the other

even in our fear
we are alike

The Wall

the room is dark

       I cannot see

I am blinded by the blackness
of your disapproval
and I cannot see .. there is no light

yet, even blind, in darkness
I would leap over this wall

I would leap, as lizards leap
or kangaroos, when danger threatens
but multiplied a thousand times

               to reach you
on the other side

no! I will not leap over this wall
    what if I should fall
    on the cutting edge of your ridicule?

oh! I am so afraid of falling
    with your arms ... not there to catch me

  they are folded across your chest
        your arms
  in firm, unyielding resolution

           your arms, your arms

your arms ... that held me tightly
centuries ago

     .. last night

Eclipse of the Sun

the sky is falling . .

ripping all our rainbows
into tattered shreds of grey

no rain   bows

only bows of rain, arched with pain
and shooting boomeranging arrows
poison dipped

from the quiver of my heart
back into myself, with deadly aim

for I remember, once you said
when *you* had wounded *me:*

"oh darling, how can hurting you
do anything but hurt me too?"

yes . . it's true, it's true

when you are hungry, I am empty
when I cry, your own tears flow
when you are cut, I bleed
when I am thirsty, you crave water
when you reach out in loneliness
I ache with need
as lonely, then, as you

even as we tear ourselves apart like this
we cannot destroy our destiny

our souls still kiss . . . ignoring us

Haste Makes Waste

when you drove away that grey and ominous day
without a single backward glance
or even a Howard Hughes rain check for tomorrow

you left behind

    your size eleven hiking boots
             your shadow, exactly six foot two
    your Peter Pan clock
        your old grey Christmas sock
               your Tarzan yell
    your red and yellow candles
          hanging on chains from the ceiling
of your monk's meditation cell
          we used to call the Hopi Indian room
your blue cashmere sweater from Saks
         the forms for your income tax
your stuffed jungle-pride beast
         with the mane of long, curly hair
your winter coats
        your toy dolphin that floats
your fleet of bathtub sailing boats
        some forget-me-nots in the back yard
your library card .. good till the end of '73
        your electric saw, your vitamin E
a few shattered dreams
        an unspoken fear .. your Ivory soap
one unshed tear
      the torn shred of rainbow
you wore behind your left ear

your autographed book
.. and our last, long look

though you remembered to take your serpent ring
and my own gold band .. and the front door key

darling, please come back
you forgot something ..... *me*

Is It Too Late?

I guess I never told you, did I?
because I couldn't quite find the words ..

      .. about the baby birds
         who flutter their wings
      inside my breast
         when you cradle my head
      and let it rest
         against your heart

      or how your hands
         on the steering wheel of the car
      steady, so sure and wise
         sometimes cause glad-tears
      to spring into my eyes
           just because they are
      so sure of what they're doing

               ... only that

and did you know

      I like to watch
      the muscles ripple in your thighs
      when you step on the brakes, suddenly
               in traffic?

      and that the way your hair grows
      at the nape of your neck

         overwhelms me?

Don't Forget Your Passport and Your Typhoid Shots

hey, funny face!

        would you like to fly a kite with me
        or climb a watermelon hill?

        wish on some shamrocks, flip a few frisbees
        prop up the window with a stick on the sill
        or gold-spray a Jerusalem sandal?

        play a game of mental chess
        smell the dew on the grass, bottle the ocean
        or light up the sky with a candle?

        pitch some blood-tie Lincoln pennies
                  build a castle in Spain
        hide a dolphin in a haystack
        expect a miracle — or walk in the rain?

        slide up a rainbow, slip down a drain
        jump on a space ship, catch a running brook
        read a symphony, or listen to a book?

        would you like to ride a whale to Vail
        sprinkle salt on a coyote's tail
        jingle jolly holly on a San Francisco trolley
        travel to Assisi — or tumble in the snow?

    no ..

        I guess you'd rather sail off to Mexico
        mumbling mantras, like a snooty Owl
                 in a beautiful pea-green boat
        with a pink pussycat
            a jar of wheat germ and honey

and sing to a small guitar
on a quiescent quest for a rhinestone star

Bon Voyage! I wish you a montage
of every good thing
will you be returning home before spring?
that's the loveliest time of the year
                              back here

you really wouldn't enjoy it across the border
those Acapulco springs are rainy-to-freezing
and who's going to take care of you
when you're lonely and cold and sneezing?

Apathy

tears spring from surplus love
                        you said

overflowing from the wells
of naked need and consummate compassion
within the human heart

but when eyes are dry, and cannot weep

          what say you then?

how would you define these listless eyes?
are they the frosted windows
of an apathetic soul, now cold and numb
immune to even former pain ..
windows through which nothing can be seen
save endless sheets of dreary rain?

or are they dry, my eyes, tonight
because they gaze upon
a stranger's form and face before me
and that stranger has begun to bore me?

if tears stem from love
                        as you just said

then this apathy in me must be
the desert wasteland of a once pure love

          now dead

decaying, unwatered by the merciful blessing
of healing tears
choked by bitterness, strangled by lies
yet waiting, like Lazarus in his tomb
for the ringing command ..

"come forth, and rise!"

The Changeling

I once believed that loneliness and need
were the deepest agonies
Fate could bring to bear upon me
while you were gone ... and your song
was silenced for a time
            till your return

    I was wrong

        you'll never guess what's happened
        I've met your astral double

        or .. perhaps you have a twin brother
        your father and mother kept secret from you
                over the years

        a twin

        who was stolen, in infancy, from his cradle
        by a wandering band of gypsies
        because he was such a beautiful boy

            a changeling child

        like the one Titania and Oberon adopted
        on an enchanted Midsummer's night

it's true — he does exist
he lives and breathes
for I have seen him, spoken with him

        his eyes, his hair, his walk
        are so very much like yours
            his voice ... tormentingly familiar

even I, who know you best
in the beginning could discern no difference
and nearly failed to pass this karmic test

of love's identity

yet, I was blind for but the briefest moment

I soon knew
there was no way
under God's Sun
he could be you

for he is not an ancient soul
here on any mission

his soul is very new
untried

nor is it tied
to any other
as is yours to mine

he hardly ever looks at flowers
and he doesn't like to sit in the woods
for hours
his eyes are blue, not ocean green
and empty ... haunted
not silvery-wise

he eats meat ... and drinks Coors

and his cheek smells strange, not like yours at all
I was only close enough to know that .. once

when he turned, unexpectedly

somehow, he doesn't seem quite so tall
as I know you to be
if I ever stood within his arms
my ear would never rest against his heart

        as it does with you

oh! he's at least two inches shorter
than your towering six feet two

almost never gentle, tender or compassionate
he has a way of suddenly growing cold and aloof
behaving as though he believes

        he's many heavens above me

but most of all . . .

        he's completely unaware
        of how deeply

        you love me

There's a Lion in My Alphabet Soup

to amuse myself and hang in there, baby
clutching a frazzled piece of rope called hope

to kill time — which I'm beginning to believe
deserves nothing short of murder

> .. memories have nine lives
> and are not so easily killed ..

to fill the yawning abyss
you left inside

to still the song of nesting birds
outside my window

> I've been playing puzzles with words

did you know that by reversing two letters
you can turn "untied" into "united"?

and — if the Holy Ghost is an "essence" of spirit
when you remove the "c" for Christ
you're left with the word
        "Essene"

> what does that mean?

I've been thinking a lot about poetry too
these eons since you left me alone
beside a treacherous, monitored telephone

like, why should *gladness* rhyme with *sadness*?

does it follow, then, that Far Away
somehow rhymes with Home to Stay?

                    and if tomb rhymes with womb
                    then does death rhyme with birth?

what freaky creatures we are
to speak a language
in which rats spelled backwards is star

It's Spring in Colorado

I touched a newborn violet
this morning, out near the dump

as a train whistle shrieked its lonely echo
from the Cripple Creek–Victor Narrow Gauge Railroad

                    haunting the air

I was not prepared to find a violet there
among the broken glass and discarded debris
nor, when I touched
the purple velvet
of its petals
did I expect to feel futility recede
                    ... tenderness begin to tower

it was delicate and shy, my April flower
much like the rain-fresh daisies
we once held within our trembling hands
then carelessly neglected
causing them to die before their season

I touched a violet today
emerging timidly from the frozen surface
of the barren field of sorrow in my heart

and wondered if it sprang to birth
from some errant seed of need
you planted there the day you left
in all that ice and snow
gently, wisely .. somehow knowing it would grow
nourished by the rich soil of your faith
                    in Us

and One Fine Day
reach trustingly toward the   Sun
                    again

Comment on Another's Verse

you wrote a poem of profound sadness
and great beauty
stanzas of sorrow, sighing
to note that more than pain and loneliness
have passed between us since we parted
unexpectedly, on St. Valentine's Day

you wrote a poem

then, after showing it, expressionless, to me
you took your rhyme away
not allowing me an answering moment
in which to say .. oh, I agree!

immeasurably more than pain and loneliness
have passed across the shadowed void
                              of emptiness between us
since we parted, unexpectedly
                    that freezing February

for pain alone
we each are strong enough to bear
as for loneliness
it could end forever the instant we decree

but so much more than pain and loneliness
has separated you from me
                    these past eight years

we, who are indivisible, have been divided
still enmeshed and struggling within a web of lies
spun by spidery strangers
who envied us the magic we once knew

                              ... lies!

which make me seem much less than me
and you much less than you . . .
bearing little likeness to our Higher Selves

yes, so much more than simple pain
                        and ordinary lonely
have passed between us
since our love's been fast asleep
and I wondered, as I scanned your verse
if it was written by yourself

                or by another

the winter of futility it landscaped
was not . . is not . . your season

        you

who always seeks the dawn in every sunset
eternally finding hope in the hopeless
however muddled the tangle, however great the mistake

                however "too late"
                it sometimes seems

        you

who so patiently taught me
our hurting times were only dreams

                not real at all

I gazed tonight
on blank, yet achingly familiar features
now sardonically, strangely *un*-familiar
then raised my eyes
and saw no auric light around your head

but saw instead

a cloud of approaching numbness
foreboding a Macbethian brew
of *double-double*-toil-and-trouble

almost as though I gazed, in truth
upon some witch's sorcery
a doppelgänger sent to haunt me
dispatched to taunt me and to make me bleed
causing time and reality to be displaced
almost as though I faced, indeed

some mad scientist's clone
of my soul's twin

and felt a final oblivion closing in
on two so innocent of the original sin
that caused it to begin, this black
and endless night

no, I cannot see your light

and it is finished

Nature Is Chauvinistic, Like Leos

I am curiously drawn

        to this lonely Laguna spot of Earth

    huddled here like an impassive toad
    tracing pictures through the slippery seaweed
    and trying to build a tower of Truth
                  for tomorrow
    from the sand-castle memories of the past
    the present being unendurable
    senseless, unthinkable .. unending

    I sit a shivering *shiva* on this November Pacific beach
    pulled by its secrets
    as by the polarity of a magnetic amulet
    worn by a powerful High Priest of Atlantis
    now buried beneath the floor of the opposite ocean

      .. watching the green-foamed, white-bubbled surf
    kissing the shore, her lover
             .. still damp from her

    now gentle, caressing him tenderly
                     subdued
    after her violent crashing
    against his rocky strength last night

and he forgiving, as always

    the two inseparable, the surf and shore

        macrocosmic lovers

caught up in the passionate ebb and flow
of Nature's eternal periodicity
conquering, submitting, giving, taking
and then to rest again, each
in the warm beauty of the macrocosm Sun
who permits the weaker Moon to rule the tides
for a greater purpose
never turning over his bright command
but delegating to her only a midnight authority
with constant evolutionary wisdom

                     .. as the lover shore
                          to the moody surf

    and as you to me

        ruling beast of the jungle
        arrogant Monster Cat

my soul is torn
I mourn that I was born

now half, no longer
whole, my soul

    needs

my soul pleads
come back!

my soul bleeds
in widow's weeds
dressed black

my soul screams

it clings to dreams
where no light gleams
in darkness

last night I dreamed
I cradled his head
in my arms

then he woke
looked in my eyes
and smiled

be still!
cruel-echoed chords
of music

you lie!

it was not his sleeping head
I cradled only icy stone

my Comforter is dead

... *isn't he?*

The Smokey Season

the smokey season is here once more

the calendars call it autumn
poets call it Indian summer

I wonder what the Ute tribes
in Colorado named it ?

> you would know

like you know about polygraphs and polar bears
phosphorite, phonetics and physics
as befits a man with such catholic interests

> my smaller mind
> amuses itself
> with more mundane
> and lesser matters
> of the moment

across the street, eight tousled lads
are playing "Red Rover .. let Jimmy come over"
and Jimmy breaks the line

I used to be afraid they wouldn't call my name
when I played that game .. and once

> they didn't

down the block, near the big oak tree
at the corner, where the kids park their bikes
someone has lit a smokey golden bonfire

and the scent of burning leaves
hangs heavy-heavy over my head, like some
nostalgic incense Madison Avenue would sell

                    under the name of *Déjà Vu*

    I would name it after you

Please Forward — Address Unknown

the misty sunrise season of gentle pink-gold spring
is here again

and I am lost and lonely
walking down a West End Avenue you have never walked with me

       where are you
       this soft May twilight?

I guess you're somewhere tramping through uncharted woods
exposing the genius-quotient of your multi-faceted mind
to the intricacies of ferns and spider webs
and the reproductive responses of moss and toadstools

or sailing through uncharted seas
exposing frolicking, rollicking dolphins to color film
knowing they will lose a tone or two of magic
                    in the development

maybe arguing mentally with the blind orthodoxy
of some spiritual or medical tome you're reading

       or gathering splintered shavings of stardust
       from the dome of a flying saucer
       floating toward a distant galaxy
                   and speeding silently
       past Sirius, correctly spelled Sirios
       for Isis ... anagramed within Osiris

you are smelling fresh, clean winds
cool green pine trees .. tangy splashes of salt water
or the musty-sweet pages of an ancient book

not even curious .. not even wondering how this spring breeze

                       smells to me
                       back here
       I'll tell you anyway.

    sweet peas ...

it smells like sweet peas .. and it smells like
lilacs and rain .. green grass .. sadness and gladness
                           intertwined

but mostly it smells of us .. our magic days
our violet-misty-loping-hoping days of wishing
when the world was fresh and bright and new

                     and we both knew

that miracles are real .. and dreams come true
and nothing is too wonderful to happen

                  if you really want it to

that's how it smells back here to me
how does spring smell out there to you?

            oh! I wish I could see

which uncharted woods you walk
       or which uncharted seas you're sailing through
and know how this first spring we've been apart

      feels and smells to you

Empty

while you're out there wandering on the wind

      darling

            what are you thinking
            what are you feeling
            what are you seeing
            what are you hearing
            what are you smelling?

and how can you do all those things alone
without me to do them with you?

            I ask you this, in these words
            because I read them tonight
            in a letter you wrote to me last spring

            now I send them back to you
            your own words
            with just these few more of my own

   ... there's such an emptiness beside me now
where you used to be
you left a space too large to fill
with any kind of happiness

    except your presence

Moon in Libra, Growing Old Gracefully

when I think of you

    I don't need the crutch of cigarettes or coffee
    to face the morning

when I remember you

    I scold the dogs more gently if they climb upon my bed
    against the rules

because of you

    I buy a bunch of violets every Tuesday
    when they're in season
    and bring them home, and keep them till they wither
    for no particular reason
    except that we once saw them sleeping
    near a bristlecone pine in Cripple Creek, Colorado

since knowing you

    I haven't felt it necessary
    to win each game of chess I play
    I notice lonely people more
    on holidays — like Christmas
    place no ornaments on the tree
    I like things naked . . . . . . even me

I'm more compassionate and patient with fools who bore me
even with the ones who ignore me

I take long walks
and yesterday I bought some colored chalks
to try to make a picture of a child

yet, I can't find any mention of this magic
in the songs of Solomon
the sonnets of Shakespeare
Montaigne's essays
or Walter Benton's poems

they wrote of friends
or lovers
who come together now and then
and we haven't said hello since August
or was it June?
that rainy evening ...
or was it late afternoon?

we cannot call this love
how could it be?
when we've never touched each other
and perhaps we never will
when we have only come as close
as resting elbows on a sill
and looking through the windows of an empty house
listening to the droning buzz of bees
kissing tangled clouds of baby's breath
and blue forget-me-nots
growing near a broken picket fence

    as children do, in enchanted gardens
    they half believe are haunted

nor can we call this friendship
friends share tragedies and joy by telephone or letter
our last communication was a postcard in July
why, one of us could even die
without the other knowing
in time to send some flowers to the church
or light a candle at a distance

it's like you told me once
if we never saw each other again
it wouldn't make any difference

    you didn't say it wouldn't matter
    you said it wouldn't make any difference

and did you know I understood the nuance?
it was so long ago but ...
    did you know?

February People Are Real Pals

lovers all use the same script
when they play their final scene

"Well, we almost made it, didn't we?
It's really better this way ... I'll call you someday"
    after a love affair ends
    and they know it's time they parted

with you, it was
"Can't we be friends?"

      friends?

that's how the whole thing started!

old chum, old pal, old Water Bearer buddy of mine
my comical, blundering, lost and wondering
Aquarian Valentine

Homesick, Inside-out

I just cranked up the arm of the old Edison
and put on my favorite record
                "I'll Take You Home Again, Kathleen"

      to keep me company
               while I look out the window
and watch the falling starflakes
             trim the pine tree in the back yard
with diamonds

      I always wondered
              why that song made me so
wistful, misty
         but I think I know why . . now

      I guess, because it's about a man
              who loves a woman so much
        that he knows

without ever being told
how she feels . .
what makes her hurt inside

        he notices

the tear in her eye
         and he sees how the roses
all have left her cheeks
        so he tells her tenderly
he's going to end her pain
            and take her home
to where her heart has ever been
since she was first his bonny bride

124

he's going to turn the world rightside up again
just for her .. because she belongs to him
and like the Little Prince
            he knows
a man is forever responsible
                        for what he has tamed
different from all others, unique
only because she is his

before Us

    I wept over the lyrics
                because it was so lovely, so beautiful
    to ponder such a crazy-quilt devotion
                            just to imagine
    being so deeply loved
                and protected from pain

after Us

    I cried when I played the record,
    because it made me so happy
                    to realize that I was loved
    as Kathleen was loved ... at last

    and I weep as I listen to it now
                        because I'm no longer
    your bonny bride
            the roses all have left my cheeks
    and you don't even notice

                            or care

and also because

    we won't be goin' to Ireland together, after all
    to pick starry shamrocks
                and kiss the Blarney Stone

make friends with the leprechauns
                    and run into each other's arms
laughing, through green meadows
                    and misty rains

            Fort Lauderdale and Acapulco
            are a million miles
            from emerald County Cork

I suppose, too, it makes me sad and heavy-hearted
to think that Kathleen, bein' Irish
must have had a terror of a temper, at times

sure, and she was after bein'
                    a bit of a pixilated dreamer

and probably didn't even have a driver's license

            but it never made any difference
            to *him*

            he loved her anyway

The Fish Meets the Water Bearer

for Michel and Etienne
by any other Sun Sign, name or century

we searched for each other
in the most unlikely places
among the most unlikely people

and when our paths finally crossed
it was for reasons so entangled
in our daily bread
and the usual trespasses

that we might not even have noticed
except for that faint quiver of wonder
like a passing chill from the night air

we loved

and the closest we've come to explaining why
is because it was you
                and because it was I

Afterthought

the very last thing you said
that very last time we spoke on the phone
across the measureless miles
                    from New York to California
was . .
        "thank you for loving me"

and I answered lightly
not too brightly

            "you're welcome"

how dense can I be?
why didn't I say

            "thank *you* for loving *me*"?

is that what you silently needed to hear?
you've always had a secret fear
I didn't value or cherish . . or appreciate enough

            your gift of love

but . . don't you remember that gentle December
when I was delivered into the cradle of your arms?
my very first newborn cry
was "thank you, oh! thank you for loving me"

no one ever really did
until you

and now you are gone
because I forgot to thank you

                    for the miracle
                    of loving me

Je Reviendrai

love is not always
doing what brings pleasure

love is also
doing what is good for someone
whatever the cost
        at the moment

sometimes, it's leaving
        .. for a while

and the love is shown then
in the pain given

for pain is a lesson
best learned
from the one who loves you the most

Missing

it isn't any easier, missing you in New York
just because you've never been here with me

    just now, as I passed Rockefeller Center
    and stopped to watch the flags of all nations
    fluttering in the breeze

        .. I heard your rippling brook laugh

    did I ever tell you
    you laugh like a rippling brook?

    a little later
    walking past St. Patrick's
    I cried

        because I saw a bird's nest
        that reminded me of your hair in the Sun

    sweet .. damp .. and musty

    yes, even here, where you never were
    you're always there
    I see you and hear you and feel you
    and smell you in the air

    oh! I wish I had told you, just once
    that the way your hair grows at the nape of your neck

        overwhelms me

So You Will Know

darling, funny Lion-face
sailing all alone out there

> just so you will know, if I ever have to go
> I have written for you, not a poem

> > but a prayer

> I will hide it softly, like a secret
> here in our enchanted, spectrum-prismed house
> so maybe someday you will find it
> and understand, then, the way I love you

> > how deep .. and why

> I hope it doesn't make you cry
> for perhaps we'll never have to say goodbye
> but will leave this Earth together
> like you promised .. that time in your letter

until then

> when I lay me lonesome
> down to sleep
> I say this sunrise prayer

> God bless the silent planet Saturn in you
> with its rays of silvery-wise
> that shine out tiny stars to guide me
> from the windows of my soul .. your eyes

God bless the baby in you
                    the small boy, fishing
the man of passion
who gentles me and trembles me
and the other, holy one

God bless each and every you
within your temple, living there
each other half of every me
                    all those I know, and knew
which, when joined together
become the always and eternal Us

    the Forever-me-of-you

that makes your heart reach out to mine
and mine to yours
across an ocean or a room
to pull us back into each other
even when we've torn ourselves so far apart
that I look up to wish for you
                    upon the midday Sun, at noon
at the same time you look up to wish for me
upon the midnight Moon

God bless your hair and skin perfume
so well remembered, memorized
from centuries of touching, trusting you
                    my own twin soul
that tells me you are home
enfolded in the circle of my arms
complete, then
with all your scattered pieces whole

so, when I lay me lonesome down to sleep
I pray to you my soul to keep
asking you to keep it safe
all through our stormy, Earth-lived night

but, if I should die before I wake
I'll pray to Him my soul to take
while I'm all alone and frightened, lost
till I find my way back home to you
and hear your chord of music
calling me through Time and Space
then smell your cheek and touch your face
and tumble back inside your arms
                    once again, Forevermore

    Amen

Across the Room

(on some lines by Leah Bodine Drake in her book)

lie near me now ... across the room
as gently as the Moon's cool glow lies upon my cheek
touch me with undemanding hands
                          as softly as a breeze of spring
might touch the petals of a violet
that almost died from winter's lingering frost

lie close to me ... across the room
possess me with a glance as silent as a windless shower
falling on a sleeping lilac blossom

lie with your arms around me ... across the room
encircling all our sorrows
                          stroke my hair, and bless me
with your slow, familiar smile
                          .. for yet a while

lie pressed against my breast ... across the room
a moment longer, slowly
                  for days, perhaps .. or months .. or years

with inexpressible atonement,
kiss away the tears
that tremble in me still,
                  until their silver streaks of pain
are erased by longing .. then fade into
                                    forgetfulness

wait yet a longer while
                  in the starlit stillness
and the purple shadows

for hate and hurt must die
if love's to be reborn anew

lie close to me .. across the room
embrace me only with the tender promise
of eternities of patience ... in your eyes

        until once more the lightning flashes
through the empty space between us
            illuminating separation's darkness

"oh, lie still ... lie so! ..

before the winds of passion start

    and the great storms shake the heart"

And Our Cup Runneth Over

my need has never been greater

it almost equals my apathy

well, do you expect an endless faith
in this bottomless grail of searching? I've been waiting
nearly eight-years-from-Forever, you know

do you know?

the poets claim you do .. that you've been waiting as long
for my song as I for yours
and my heart believes them, when my mind is fast asleep
but when did a poet ever win a ball game in the final inning?

out of habit, I wonder how and when .. I shall discover you
or will it be a rediscovery?
within what midnight dream .. blazed by which flashing comet
chorded by which symphony's crashing notes

or silently, on a clear day?

in what spot on which map .. will we consummate our reunion
Colorado-deep .. Vermont-snowy .. Arizona-Indian-haunted
Ohio-dotted-with-baby-lambs-and-daffodils

or California-earthquaked?

I left no trail of twisted twigs for you to follow
that I remember .. perhaps a winding path of wild blueberries
eaten eons ago by hungry birds of Time
did you make, for me, a mound of stones or pebbles

marked with your initials or a cross

I think not

we could meet, I suppose, on a Manhattan subway, reaching up
for the same chrome handle .. in a weaving car
too narrow to avoid the electrical shock of our auras blending

                              but what would you
                              be doing there ?

        Denver is more likely

                  or Vail in winter, coated white

I might find you on a Sunday morning .. before the early mass
lighting a lone Francescan candle in St. Patrick's

standing hesitant, on a deserted grassy knoll in Dallas
though why in God's name I'd ever go to Dallas, I don't know

maybe walking, hunched over, amnesia-like
along some sinister street .. in Rochester, New York
but .. why should Fate arrange for us to meet
within the nightmare of such a debt of pain .. already paid ?

on All Hallow's Eve, in costume ? ... me masquerading as happy
you, dressed simply as you .. will you tear off my mask
with your deep knowing gaze ... again ?

I'd like our happening to be in a lilting place, like Holland
high on some windswept hill, blowing tulips pink, sky-blue
                                        and yellow

or near a sweet, spring-scented lilac bush

our coming together could be accompanied
by the chiming of Big Ben, in London
and the Changing-of-the-Guards

or in the moonlight .. beneath the grieving shadow
of the Great Pyramid of Giza, trembling
at our unexpected presence there
                    so near its mystery

perhaps in the Egyptian room ... of the musty British Museum
running through the Scottish heather
                    or in Ireland, through the shamrocks
disembarking from a ship .. on the stormy coast of Wales

                    I'm not much of a traveler

though I might, someday, be near an ocean .. even if not beyond i
so it could be a trash and bottle-littered shore
in Laguna or San Luis Obispo .. please, God, not Newport Beach

with some other lost ones playing soft guitar
to the rhythm of your walk, approaching ...
I'll look up
exactly as a sea gull swirls above your head
and your body, turning so to watch its flight
will stab my soul with its familiar posture

            will your hair be dark
            or sunlight gold?

it will be growing cold, along the water's edge
you'll offer me your sweater

                    I will smile

what if we should pass, hurried and harried
in some crowded store .. what matter what city, which store?
our minds too intent on nothing
to feel the organ music in our hearts
                    pounding annunciation hosannas
as we drown beneath a sea of strange, blank faces

unseen, unheard?

of all these places engraved and blessed by my images of us
for some reason I can't seem to explain
the one that ever chords
the clearest precognitive music in my heart

      is an airport, in the rain

but that requires synchronization
of an airline's scheduled flight

            and our meeting is not timed

      only preordained

on the astral level
of our Higher Selves
are there clocks?

      no appointed hour has been set to guide us

         like daybreak

    5:01 P.M. quitting time

  high noon

         a sunset angelus

   or twelve o'clock midnight

beneath a street lamp's golden glow
      starflakes falling all around us
bells wildly ringing in .. which brand New Year?
right here .. in this unsuspecting, quiet town

       where I have waited

or will we finally awaken from our dream of separation
in some lavender-crystalled twilight

　　　　　　　　on another, brighter star

and weep to know we missed each other
down here, on this lonely one

beautiful in recognition .. draped in promised miracles
but without flesh bodies, with which to sing our love

　　　　　　how then, can I enter
　　　　　　the deep-deep-cool-green woods of you

　　　　　　or you fill the empty caverns of me?

12th House Affliction

I must go now

        don't hold me with your eyes
        and reach your heart across the room like that

            or my own will break

        love you?
        of course I love you
        that's why I have to go, before you know

            how much

tomorrow, I'll be stronger
and we'll walk up to the Garden of the Gods again
        and look for Indian arrowheads

            for luck

Pluto Conjunct Venus

close your ears to the sound of my voice
and through the thunder of a thousand cannons
you will hear it calling your name

blind yourself to the light in my eyes
and through the blackness of eternal night
you will feel them piercing your soul

insulate your body against my hands
and through blocks of ice
it will tremble in response to my touch

turn your cheek away from my breath
and through layers of rock
you will feel it hot against your lips
                                    and musty

like jungle grass

Brother Sun–Sister Moon

was it Tagore who first said:

Faith is the bird that feels the light
and sings when the dawn is dark?

maybe so, but it was Francis of Assisi
who *knew* it first

listen, Francis . . .
I heard him singing just now

                    that crazy bird

from the deep depths
of the dark night of my soul
and God knows
there's no light for him to feel
no promise, even, of a sunrise

just a few faint notes he sang
not really a morning song

poor bird, I believe he's hungry
it's been so long
since I had a crumb of caring
or a morsel of memory to feed him

    why does he sing?

doesn't he know that spring
might be planning never to return
and is almost certain
to be late again this year?

there! he warbled a cadenza!

Francesco, did you hear?

Echo of Mars Unaroused

you see?
I am still me

     the secret place inside
     where my heart will always hide
     from the withering clutch of too much need
     has not been reached

I remain myself
with courage still to face the Sun

     it's not a hollow victory I've won
       to still be me

why should I grieve?
my dreams are made of sterner stuff
and Spring will be here
       soon enough . . .

because she once told me, with her magical
laugh, *"I always read the last page first!"*
sensing, like all Geminis, that the End is
the Beginning, here then ...

in loving remembrance of

Jackie Habegger

one of the most enchanted creatures
to ever live and love in this world
or in any other